FRESH & TASTY

Quick & Easy Cooking

BARNES & NOBLE
BOOKS
NEW YORK

This edition published by Barnes & Noble, Inc.,
by arrangement with R&R Publications Marketing Pty. Ltd.

Publisher: Richard Carroll
Creative Director: Paul Sims
Production Manager: Anthony Carroll
Computer Graphics: Lucy Adams
Food Photography: Robert Monro, Warren Webb, Andrew Warn, William Meppem, Andrew Elton, Quentin Bacon, Gary Smith, Per Ericson
Food Stylists: Ann Fayle, Susan Bell, Coty Hahn, Janet Lodge, Di Kirby
Recipe Development: Ellen Argyriou, Di Kirby, Janet Lodge
Proof Reader: Cindy Brown

Includes index
ISBN 0 7607 3355 4
EAN 9 780760 733554

First edition printed March 2002
Computer Typeset in Garamond, Times New Roman & Humanist

Printed in Singapore

Contents

Introduction

The rise of fast food has seen many people scrambling to the phone in between appointments or at the end of a long working day to find a quick-fix for their hunger pangs. However, there has been a rapid rebound back to homemade cooking as people realize that there's something about food made in your own kitchen that cannot be duplicated in a commercial establishment. It tastes better, it is more satisfying, and it gives you a good feeling to know you have prepared a tasty meal for yourself and your family in the ultimate labor of love.

So the challenge for our team has been to compile a collection of recipes that are quick and easy to prepare, but take no shortcuts on taste. We believe we have achieved this tall order with outstanding variety: Soups, Salads and Starters, Meat and Poultry, Fish and Shellfish, Vegetable Dishes and Desserts and Sweet Things designed for your pure enjoyment. All of our recipes have been tried and tested by our talented team of experts so you can be sure that they will turn out exactly the way they appear in the pictures–simply sensational. Take a few moments to meander through this book because our recipes will tantalize your senses and make you eager to indulge in the next experience.

Take a straightforward Sausage Sizzle, T-Bone Steak or Lamb Satay Kebab, for example. It takes only minutes to cook them yourself and serve them fresh to your family on your own table or outside in the hot weather during a barbecue with good friends. Find out how to prepare them properly and you will avoid overcooking them or drowning them in an imbalance of seasonings that detract from the pleasure that can be given by these favorite foods. Small variations can make a world of difference between the average and the spectacular, and we can show you how to strike the right balance.

Perhaps you want to make something with an air of style and sophistication, without pouring over a hot oven for hours. Our seafood selection will surprise you because we offer unique combinations of flavors–such as Shellfish and Rocket Pizzas, and Salmon with Pineapple Salsa–all of which can be put together in the same time it takes to fry up a plate of burger and chips. But rather than walk away feeling disappointed that you have just fed your body pure fat, you can feast on a fabulous fare without regrets. We have taken all the goodness of nature and brought it into your kitchen in each recipe. Whether a wonderful Asparagus and Lemon Risotto or Beef Fillet with Wild Mushrooms, they leave a pleasant sensation in your stomach. Best of all, they are uncomplicated and help you avoid the trap of the "fast-food lifestyle."

New Confidence

Our delectable dishes leave you with the feeling that you can turn your amateur skills into the expertise of a seasoned chef. The advice given by our experts in each set of instructions are carefully considered so that you get the result you seek with minimum effort. You will attack each page of this cookbook with enthusiasm as you embark on this journey of creative cuisine. You will start to gain the knowledge of how ingredients work together to take on a whole new appearance and a bold new taste.

Best of all, you will gain a new confidence when hosting guests because you know that you can still treat them to a wonderful meal and still spend the majority of your time enjoying their presence. No more running around behind the scenes to present to them a seemingly effortless three-course meal. No more wondering whether what you see in cookbook images is really the reward for your effort. We take the stress out of hosting, and ensure you make it a frequent occasion. Cooking need not be complicated when you have our recipes at your fingertips.

From starter to dessert, we have every course covered. Try various combinations on your family and friends and you will start to hear more and more compliments come your way. Sometimes sticking to old favorites can be comforting, but why not splash out and try something out of the ordinary? For instance, start with Chicken and Corn Chowder, move onto Pork Chops with Chili Rice and Glazed Apples, and top it off with Mini Chocolate Muffins with Mocha Sauce. Or perhaps you might like some other combination, such as Beetroot, Pear and Bitter Leaf Salad, Fresh Crab Tagliatelle and Raspberry and Elderflower Fool. The possibilities are limited only by your willingness to move away from the mundane towards something more appealing.

So we wish you nothing less than bliss from this book. It is our absolute pleasure to take the burden out of homemade meals and make delicious delights accessible to even the person most pressed for time. This book will spare you from all guilt of money spent on expensive restaurant meals and fat-filled fast food, and bring many friends to your door in the pursuit of good food and great company.

Enjoy!

Soups, Salads, and Starters

There's no need to forsake the pleasure of homemade cooking in favor of a busy lifestyle if you know how to make a scrumptious soup, salad, or starter in just minutes. Our compilation of recipes will ensure that you avoid the traps of take-out meals that are loaded with calories and chip away at your good intentions to save for more important things. From the goodness of a Greek Salad to the simple pleasure of Coconut, Sweet Potato, and Spinach Soup, this cookbook will firm your resolve to enjoy nothing less than the best of our quick and easy cuisine.

Coconut, Sweet Potato, and Spinach Soup

Note: Sweet potatoes have a slightly nutty flavor. They also make the texture of this coconut soup really creamy. For a fantastic light meal, serve the soup with naan bread.

2 tbsp butter
1 lb sweet potatoes, cut into $^1/_2$ in dice
1 onion, chopped
2 cloves garlic, crushed
1 tsp grated fresh root ginger
1 tbsp medium curry paste
2$^1/_2$ cups vegetable stock
1 cup coconut milk
juice of 1 lime
$^1/_2$ tsp dried crushed chilies
3 cups fresh spinach, shredded
salt and black pepper

1 Melt the butter in a saucepan and fry the potatoes, onion, garlic, ginger, and curry paste for 5 minutes, or until lightly golden.

2 Add the stock, coconut milk, lime juice and chili. Bring to the boil, cover and simmer for 15 minutes or until the potatoes are tender.

3 Leave the soup to cool a little, then purée half of it with a hand blender. Return the purée to the pan, add the spinach and cook for 1-2 minutes, until the spinach has just wilted and the soup has heated through. Season to taste.

Serves 4
Preparation 10 mins
Cooking 25 mins
Calories 289
Fat 4g

Griddled Scallops with Orange Salsa

2 small oranges
4 sun-dried tomatoes in oil, drained and chopped
1 clove garlic, crushed
1 tbsp balsamic vinegar
4 tbsp extra virgin olive oil
salt and black pepper
1 large head fennel, cut lengthways into 8 slices
12 fresh prepared scallops
4 tbsp crème fraîche
rocket leaves to serve

1 Slice the top and bottom off 1 of the oranges, then cut away the peel and pith, following the curve of the fruit. Cut between the membranes to release the segments, then chop roughly. Squeeze the juice of the other orange into a bowl, add the chopped orange, tomatoes, garlic, vinegar, and 3 tablespoons of the oil, then season.

2 Heat a ridged cast-iron grill pan or heavy-based frying pan. Brush both sides of each fennel slice with half the remaining oil. Cook for 2-3 minutes on each side, until tender and charred. Transfer to serving plates and keep warm.

3 Brush the scallops with the remaining oil and cook for 1 minute, then turn and cook for 30 seconds or until cooked through. Top the fennel with 1 tablespoon of crème fraîche, 3 scallops, and the salsa. Serve with the rocket.

Note: Peppery rocket and an orange salsa bring out the best in the succulent scallops in this luxurious but quick dish. It makes a great starter or a light, refreshing main course.

Serves 4
Preparation 12 mins
Cooking 10 mins
Calories 321
Fat 6g

Pikelets with Smoked Salmon and Horseradish

Note: Pikelets are small batter pancakes similar to Russian blinis. Their texture makes them perfect partners for smoked salmon and creamy horseradish.

Serves 4
Preparation 10 mins
Cooking 5 mins
Calories 290
Fat 4g

1/2 cup crème fraîche
1 tbsp creamed horseradish
1 tbsp chopped fresh dill, plus extra to garnish
squeeze of fresh lemon juice
1/2 tsp clear honey
salt and black pepper
8 pikelets
1/2 lb smoked salmon slices

1 Preheat the grill to high. In a bowl, combine the crème fraîche, horseradish, dill, lemon juice, and honey, then season.

2 Toast the pikelets under the grill for 1-2 minutes, until golden, then turn them over and cook for a further 1-2 minutes. Top each pikelet with a spoonful of the crème fraîche mixture, some smoked salmon, and a sprinkling of black pepper. Serve garnished with dill.

Greek Salad

1 lettuce, leaves separated and shredded
2 tomatoes, sliced
1 small cucumber, sliced
1 red bell pepper, cut into thin strips
1 small onion, thinly sliced
1 cup feta cheese, cut into small cubes
12 black olives

Lemon and Mint Dressing
6 tbsp olive oil
2 tbsp lemon juice
2 tsp chopped fresh mint
2 tsp chopped fresh marjoram

1 Line a large serving platter or salad bowl with lettuce. Top with tomatoes, cucumber, red bell pepper, onion, feta cheese, and olives.

2 Dressing: Place oil, lemon juice, mint, and marjoram in a screwtop jar. Season to taste. Shake well. Spoon over salad. Serve immediately.

Serves 4
Preparation 10 mins
Cooking nil
Calories 360
Fat 9g

Carrot and Sweet Potato Soup

Serves 4
Preparation 10 mins
Cooking 40 mins
Calories 276
Fat 4g

2 tbsp butter
1 large onion, chopped
3 large carrots, chopped
1 large sweet potato, chopped
4 cups chicken or vegetable stock
$^3/_4$ cup sour cream
2 tbsp chopped fresh dill

1 Melt butter in a saucepan over a medium heat. Add onion, carrots, and sweet potato. Cook for five minutes.

2 Stir in stock. Bring to a boil. Simmer for 30 minutes. Cool slightly.

3 Puree soup. Return soup to a clean saucepan. Stir in sour cream. Cook, without boiling and stirring constantly, for 5 minutes or until soup is hot. Stir in dill. Serve immediately.

Chicken and Corn Chowder

Note: To chop the sweet corn, place in a food processor or blender and process using the pulse button until the sweet corn is coarsely chopped. Creamed sweet corn can be used in place of the kernels if you wish. If using creamed sweet corn there is no need to chop it.

Serves 6
Preparation 10 mins
Cooking 30 mins
Calories 320
Fat 6g

1 tbsp vegetable oil
1 small onion, diced
1/2 lb boneless chicken breast fillets, shredded
3 potatoes, chopped
3 cups chicken stock
1 1/2 cups canned sweet corn kernels, drained and chopped
1 1/4 cups milk
1 bay leaf
freshly ground black pepper
1 tbsp lemon juice
2 tbsp chopped, fresh parsley
1 tbsp snipped fresh chives
1/2 cup grated Parmesan cheese

1 Heat oil in a saucepan over a medium heat, add onion and cook, stirring, for 4-5 minutes or until onion is soft. Add chicken and cook for 2 minutes longer or until chicken just changes color.

2 Add potatoes and stock and bring to a boil. Reduce heat and simmer for 10 minutes or until potatoes are almost cooked. Stir sweet corn, milk, bay leaf, and black pepper to taste into stock mixture and bring to a boil. Reduce heat and simmer for 3-4 minutes or until potatoes are cooked. Remove bay leaf. Stir in lemon juice, parsley, chives, and black pepper to taste. Just prior to serving, sprinkle with Parmesan cheese.

Gnocchi with Mascarpone and Blue Cheese

Note: Creamy mascarpone and gorgonzola produce this meltingly good Italian gnocchi dish. It needs to be served with a lightly dressed green or mixed salad.

Serves 4
Preparation 5 mins
Cooking 10 mins
Calories 460
Fat 8g

14 oz pack fresh gnocchi
1 tbsp pine nut kernels
1/2 cup mascarpone
1 cup gorgonzola cheese, crumbled
salt and black pepper

1 Cook the gnocchi according to the packet instructions. Drain well, then transfer to a shallow flameproof dish.

2 Preheat the grill to high. Place the pine nut kernels in the grill pan and toast for 2-3 minutes, stirring from time to time, until golden. Keep an eye on them as they can burn quickly.

3 Meanwhile, put the mascarpone and gorgonzola cheese in a saucepan and warm over a very low heat, stirring, until melted. Season to taste. Spoon over the gnocchi, then grill for 2-3 minutes, until bubbling and golden. Scatter over the pine nut kernels and serve.

Beetroot, Pear, and Bitter Leaf Salad

½ cup walnut pieces
½ lb mixed salad leaves, including radicchio and frisée
½ lb cooked beetroot in natural juices, sliced
2 pears, quartered, cored, sliced
1½oz Parmesan
fresh chives to garnish

Dressing
2 tbsp chopped fresh herbs, including basil, chives, mint, and parsley
4 tbsp walnut oil
2 tbsp extra virgin olive oil
1 clove garlic, crushed
2 tsp red wine vinegar
1 tsp clear honey
salt and black pepper

1 Preheat the grill to high. To make the dressing, blend the herbs, walnut oil, olive oil, garlic, vinegar, and honey until smooth in a food processor or with a hand blender. Season to taste.

2 Place the walnuts on a baking sheet and grill for 2-3 minutes, until golden, turning often. Arrange the leaves, beetroot, and pear slices on serving plates. Scatter over the walnuts, then shave over thin slivers of Parmesan, using a vegetable peeler. Spoon the dressing over the salad and garnish with whole chives.

Note: Slightly bitter radicchio and frisée leaves are set off by sweet beetroot and pears. If preparing the salad ahead of time, toss the pears in lemon juice to stop them browning.

Serves 4
Preparation 15 mins
Cooking 5 mins
Calories 354
Fat 8g

Tomato and Mozzarella Salad

Note: This classic Italian salad never fails to please and the hot dressing works really well with it. Don't skimp on the fresh basil or balsamic vinegar – it won't be the same.

Serves 4
Preparation 10 mins
Cooking 5 mins
Calories 306
Fat 7g

6 plum tomatoes, sliced
1 cup mozzarella, drained and sliced
2 spring onions, sliced
6 tbsp black olives
salt and black pepper

Dressing
3 tbsp extra virgin olive oil
1 clove garlic, crushed
2 tsp balsamic vinegar
2 tbsp chopped fresh basil

1 Arrange the tomatoes, mozzarella, spring onions and olives in layers on serving plates and season.

2 To make the dressing, heat the oil and garlic in a small saucepan over a very low heat for 2 minutes or until the garlic has softened but not browned. Remove the pan from the heat, add the vinegar and basil, then pour over the salad.

Clam and Black Mussel Broth

3 tbsp vegetable oil
1 onion finely chopped
2 tbsp Tom Yum paste
$^1/_2$ lb surf clams, cleaned and sandless
$^1/_2$ lb black mussels, cleaned
1 cup chicken stock
1 stalk lemon grass, chopped
juice of one lime
1 tbsp fresh cilantro leaves, roughly chopped
1 tbsp cilantro stalk and roots, finely chopped
1 tbsp Thai fish sauce
3 cups chicken stock

1 Heat oil in a wok or large cooking pot. Add onion, Tom Yum, clams, and mussels. Simmer, covered with a lid for 30 seconds.
2 Add chicken stock, lemon grass, lime juice, cilantro stalk and roots, Thai fish sauce and stir through. Cook until all shells have opened.
3 Add fresh cilantro leaves and serve in soup bowls.

Serves 6
Preparation 10 mins
Cooking 40 mins
Calories 133
Fat <1g

Caesar Salad with Crispy Prosciutto

OVEN TEMPERATURE
400°F, 200°C, GAS 6

Note: Even classic Caesar salad can be improved upon. Here, grilled prosciutto adds extra crunch–and a dash of Worcestershire sauce peps up the traditional dressing.

Serves 4
Preparation 15 mins
Cooking 15 mins
Calories 313
Fat 5g

2 1/2 in slices day-old bread, cut into 1/2 in cubes
4 large slices prosciutto
2 cos or romaine lettuces, torn into bite-sized pieces
1/2 cup Parmesan, grated, plus extra to serve (optional)

Dressing
8 anchovies, drained and mashed
2 tbsp extra virgin olive oil
3 tbsp reduced calorie mayonnaise
1 clove garlic, crushed
1 tsp white wine vinegar
1/2 tsp Worcestershire sauce
black pepper

1 Preheat the oven. To make the croûtons, place the bread cubes on a baking tray and cook for 10-12 minutes, until crisp and golden, turning occasionally.
2 Preheat the grill to high. Grill the prosciutto for 1 minute or until very crisp, then leave to cool for 2 minutes. Place the lettuce leaves, croûtons and Parmesan in a bowl.
3 To make the dressing, put the anchovies, oil, mayonnaise, garlic, vinegar, Worcestershire sauce, and black pepper into a bowl and whisk until smooth. Spoon over the lettuce and croûtons, then toss until well coated. Top with the crispy prosciutto and extra Parmesan, if using.

Vine Tomatoes and Goat's Cheese Bruschetta

1 lb small vine-ripened tomatoes
2 tbsp extra virgin olive oil
1 clove garlic, crushed
4 sprigs fresh thyme
4 thick slices ciabatta, cut on the diagonal
4 tbsp ready-made tapenade
$^1/_2$ cup soft goat's cheese, cut into chunks
fresh basil leaves to garnish

1 Preheat the oven. Place the tomatoes, still on the vine, in a roasting tin and drizzle over the oil. Scatter over the garlic and thyme sprigs. Roast for 15 minutes or until the tomatoes are tender. Divide the tomatoes into 4 portions of roughly the same size, each still attached to part of the vine.

2 Meanwhile, preheat the grill to high. Toast the bread on both sides until golden. Spread each slice with 1 tablespoon of tapenade, add a few chunks of goat's cheese, and top with the tomatoes on the vine. Drizzle over the juices from the roasting tin and sprinkle with the basil leaves.

OVEN TEMPERATURE
425°F, 220°C, GAS 7

Note: The tapenade in this dish is full of strong Mediterranean flavors–capers, anchovies and olives. You can use loose cherry tomatoes, but cook them for a few minutes less.

Serves 4
Preparation 10 mins
Cooking 20 mins
Calories 278
Fat 6g

Meat and Poultry

Take a trip to your local butcher with our serving suggestions in mind and you will be delighted how you can put together a delectable dish with minimum effort and maximum results. From Cajun cutlets to teriyaki tenderloins, meat and poultry tossed with seasonings is thoroughly enjoyable and so simple to prepare. Whether to add a exciting element to a barbecue with friends or to surprise your family with a tasty new dish, take a browse through the following pages for inspiration. You will be forever convinced that you can balance your work commitments with your love of homemade cooking, and enjoy the best that both worlds have to offer.

Lamb with Mint Butter and Saffron Mash

Note: Creamy saffron mash and mint butter turn juicy lamb steaks into a wonderful meal. The only other thing you need are some fresh green vegetables.

Serves 4
Preparation 10 mins plus 5 mins standing and 5 mins resting
Calories 808
Fat 7g

2 lb floury potatoes, such as Desirée or King Edward, cut into chunks
salt and black pepper
2 tbsp butter, softened
2 tbsp chopped fresh mint, plus extra leaves to garnish
1/2 tsp ground cumin
4 tbsp single cream
pinch of saffron strands
4 lamb leg steaks

1 Cook the potatoes in a large saucepan of lightly salted water for 15 minutes or until tender. Meanwhile, mash together half of the butter, the mint, cumin and a little pepper, then cover and refrigerate. Put the cream and saffron strands in a small pan, gently heat through, then remove from the heat and set aside for 5 minutes to infuse.

2 Preheat the grill to high. Season the lamb steaks and grill for 4-5 minutes on each side, or until cooked to your liking. Cover with foil and leave to rest for 5 minutes. Meanwhile, drain the potatoes well and mash with a potato masher, then mix in the remaining butter and the saffron cream and season.

3 Divide the chilled mint butter between the steaks and grill for a few seconds until it melts. Serve the steaks with the saffron mash and any pan juices. Garnish with mint.

Spiced Pork with Humous and Cilantro Oil

4 pork fillets, about 1/2 lb each
1 tbsp olive oil
1 tsp paprika
1/2 tsp cayenne pepper
10oz tub of fresh humous
lemon wedges to serve
fresh cilantro to garnish

Cilantro Oil
4 tbsp extra virgin olive oil
2 spring onions, finely chopped
1 tbsp chopped fresh cilantro
salt and black pepper

1 Preheat the oven. Wipe the pork with damp kitchen towels. Mix the oil with the paprika and cayenne pepper. Rub over the pork fillets.

2 Heat a heavy-based frying pan, add the pork and fry for 2 minutes, turning until seared all over. Add 2 tablespoons of water, cover and simmer for 10 minutes. Remove from the heat and set aside for 5 minutes. Put the humous into a baking dish and place in the oven for 10 minutes to heat through.

3 Meanwhile, make the cilantro oil. Heat the oil in a small pan, add the onions and cilantro and cook for 3-4 minutes, until the onions have softened. Cool slightly, season, then blend until fairly smooth in a food processor or with a hand blender. Serve the pork in slices with the humous, cilantro oil, and lemon wedges. Garnish with cilantro.

OVEN TEMPERATURE
350°F, 180°C, GAS 4

Note: The sunny flavors of the Mediterranean have inspired this pork dish, served with baked humous and drizzled with cilantro (coriander)–flavored oil. It's good with pita bread.

Serves 4
Preparation 10 mins plus 5 mins standing
Calories 548
Fat 9g

Honeyed Gammon with Pineapple Salsa

Note: This is not the usual version of gammon and pineapple! A spicy pineapple salsa really sets gammon steaks alight. Serve with either rice or potatoes and a fresh green salad.

Serves 4
Preparation 15 mins
Cooking 10 mins
Calories 535
Fat 6g

4 thick smoked gammon steaks, about 1/2 lb each
2 sprigs fresh thyme
1 tbsp clear honey
lime wedges to serve and fresh cilantro to garnish

Salsa
2 tomatoes
1/2 lb pineapple, cut into 1/2 inch cubes
1 clove garlic, crushed
1 red chili, deseeded and chopped
2 tbsp extra virgin olive oil
juice of 1/2 lime
2 tbsp chopped fresh cilantro
salt and black pepper

1 First make the salsa. Put the tomatoes in a bowl and cover with boiling water. Leave for 30 seconds, then skin, deseed, and dice. Combine with the pineapple, garlic, chili, oil, lime juice, and cilantro. Season to taste and set aside.

2 Preheat the grill to high. Score the fat around the edge of each steak and rub all over with the thyme sprigs. Brush with honey and grill the gammon for 2-3 minutes on each side, until tender and cooked through. Serve with the salsa and lime wedges, garnished with cilantro.

Beef Fillet with Wild Mushrooms

1/2 oz dried porcini mushrooms
6 tbsp butter
4 beef fillet steaks
3 cups mixed fresh wild mushrooms, sliced
1 clove garlic, crushed
1 tsp chopped fresh thyme, plus extra to garnish
1/2 cup red wine
1/2 cup beef stock
salt and black pepper

1 Preheat the oven. Cover the dried mushrooms with 3 fl oz of boiling water. Soak for 15 minutes or until softened. Strain, reserving the soaking liquid, then chop the mushrooms. Melt 1/2 tablespoon of the butter and fry the steaks for 2-3 minutes on each side, until browned. Wrap loosely in foil and keep warm in the oven.

2 Add 1/2 tablespoon of the butter to the pan and fry the fresh mushrooms, dried mushrooms, garlic and thyme for 4 minutes or until the fresh mushrooms have softened. Add the wine, increase the heat and boil for 1-2 minutes, until the sauce has reduced by half.

3 Mix the dried mushroom soaking liquid with the beef stock, then add to the pan and simmer for 3 minutes. Stir in the remaining butter and season. Serve with the steaks, garnished with thyme.

OVEN TEMPERATURE
325°F, 160°C, GAS 3

Note: Fillet steak, red wine and mushrooms is a much-loved combination. Here, both dried and fresh mushrooms are used to give the sauce a really intense flavor.

Serves 4
Preparation 10 mins plus 15 mins soaking
Cooking 20 mins
Calories 436
Fat 6g

Chicken Parcels with Tarragon Cream Sauce

OVEN TEMPERATURE
400°F, 200°C, GAS 6

Note: It's a surprise when you cut into these chicken breasts and discover a delicious filling of sun-dried tomatoes. The rich sauce and baby leeks are perfect accompaniments.

Serves 4
Preparation 10 mins
Cooking 35 mins
Calories 545
Fat 8g

4 large skinless boneless chicken breasts
8 sun-dried tomatoes in oil, drained
8 rashers rindless smoked bacon
2 tbsp olive oil
1 lb baby leeks
1 1/2 cups fresh chicken stock
2 tbsp brandy
2/3 cup carton single cream
2 tbsp chopped fresh tarragon, plus extra to garnish
salt and black pepper

1 Preheat the oven. Cut a deep slice into one side of each chicken breast to make a pocket. Place 2 sun-dried tomatoes in each pocket, then wrap 2 bacon rashers around each breast. Secure with wetted cocktail sticks.
2 Heat 1 tablespoon of the oil in an ovenproof frying pan. Cook the chicken for 2-3 minutes, turning once, until browned all over. Transfer to the oven and cook for 15 minutes or until the chicken is cooked through. Transfer to a plate, remove the cocktail sticks and keep warm. Meanwhile, preheat the grill to high. Brush the leeks with the remaining oil and grill for 6-8 minutes, until softened.
3 Meanwhile, add the stock and brandy to the frying pan. Cook over a high heat for 3 minutes, stirring and scraping, until reduced by half. Whisk in the cream and tarragon and simmer for 2-3 minutes, until slightly thickened. Season, then spoon over the chicken parcels and leeks. Garnish with tarragon.

Balsamic Duck Breasts with Potato Röstis

2 tbsp balsamic vinegar
1 tsp clear honey
1 clove garlic, crushed
pinch of Chinese five-spice powder
salt and black pepper
4 boneless duck breasts, about 6 oz each
1 lb waxy potatoes, such as Charlotte, peeled and grated
2 tbsp butter
2 tbsp olive oil
4 tbsp apple and plum chutney to serve
fresh herbs, such as marjoram or basil, to garnish

1 Combine the vinegar, honey, garlic, Chinese spices, salt and pepper in a bowl. Cut several slashes in each duck breast with a sharp knife and rub in the mixture. Set aside.

2 Rinse the grated potatoes, squeeze dry in a clean tea towel, then season. Heat 1/2 oz butter and 1 tablespoon of the oil in a frying pan, add 4 tablespoons of the mixture (about half) and press down gently to make 4 röstis. Fry for 5-6 minutes on each side, until browned and cooked through. Repeat to make 4 more.

3 Meanwhile, preheat the grill to high. Cook the duck close to the heat for 3-4 minutes on each side, until charred. Wrap in foil and leave to rest for 5 minutes, then slice it and serve with any juices, the röstis, and spoonfuls of chutney. Garnish with the fresh herbs.

Note: A sweet and sour apple and plum chutney cuts right through the richness of the duck, and the crispy potato pancakes help to bring all the intense flavors together.

Serves 4
Preparation 10 mins
Cooking 30 mins
Calories 460
Fat 7g

Serves 4 **Preparation** 6 mins **Cooking** 12 mins **Calories** 900 **Fat** 11g

Quick Sausage Sizzle

Note: This method is suitable for cooking a large number of sausages to serve around. Pork or beef thick sausages are used, which are simmered in water before placing on the barbecue. This prevents the thick sausages from splitting and reduces cooking time. Calculate the amount of sausages needed for the number of people to be served.

4lb pork or beef sausages
2lb onions, thinly sliced

Honey and Chili Marinade
1/4 cup red wine
1/2 cup honey
1/4 tsp ground chili

1 To make marinade, mix all ingredients together.

2 Place sausages in a large saucepan and cover with cold water. Heat slowly until simmering point is reached, then simmer for 5 minutes. Drain well. If not required immediately refrigerate until needed.

3 Heat the barbecue until hot and grease grill bars with oil. Pour the honey and chili marinade into a heatproof bowl and place at the side of the barbecue. Arrange sausages from left to right on the grill bars or hotplate and brush with the marinade. Turn and brush with marinade after one minute and continue turning and basting for 10 minutes until sausages are well glazed and cook through. Give a final brushing with marinade as they are removed to a serving platter.

4 To cook onions, oil the hot plate and place on the onion slices. Toss at intervals, drizzle with a little oil as they cook. Serve the honey and glazed sausages with the onions and accompany with salad and garlic bread.

Lamb Satays

Serves Yields approximately 30 skewers
Preparation 10 mins
Cooking 10 mins plus marinating
Calories 113 each skewer
Fat 2g each skewer

4 lb boned shoulder of lamb
wooden skewers

Satay Marinade
1/2 cup peanut butter
1/2 tsp chili powder
1/2 tsp ground ginger
2 tbsp lemon juice
1 tbsp brown sugar
1/2 cup coconut milk

Dipping Sauce
1/4 cup satay marinade

1 For the marinade, place all ingredients in a pan, heat and stir to combine.

2 Cut the lamb into 1/5 in cubes. Place into a non-metal bowl and stir in 6 fl oz of marinade. Cover and marinate for half to one hour, or longer in the refrigerator.

3 Soak the skewers in hot water for 1/2 hour.

4 Thread 2 or 3 lamb strips onto each skewer, using a weaving action. Spread to cover 2/3 of the skewer only.

5 Heat barbecue until hot. Place an overturned wire-cake rack over grill bars to prevent marinade charring the hot grill. Arrange the skewers in rows on the wire rack and cook for approximately 8-10 minutes, turning frequently. Brush remaining marinade from the bowl over the lamb during cooking.

6 Thin down the remaining marinade with extra coconut milk, place in a heatproof bowl and heat on the barbecue. Remove skewers to a platter and drizzle immediately with the heated marinade.

Cajun Cutlets

Serves 3-4
Preparation 10 mins
Cooking 8 mins
Calories 696
Fat 28g

6 tbsp butter
3 tsp Cajun seasoning
1 small red chili, seeded and chopped
12 lamb cutlets
1 tbsp olive oil

1 Beat the butter to soften and mix in $1^1/_2$ teaspoons of the Cajun seasoning and the chopped chili. Place butter along the center of a piece of plastic wrap or greaseproof paper to one centimeter thickness. Fold plastic wrap over the butter then roll up. Smooth into a sausage shape and twist ends. Refrigerate to firm.

2 Trim the cutlets if necessary and snip the membrane at the side to prevent curling. Flatten slightly with the side of a meat mallet. Mix together $1^1/_2$ teaspoons of the Cajun seasoning and olive oil then rub mixture well into both sides of the cutlets. Place in a single layer onto a tray, cover and stand 20 minutes at room temperature, or longer in the refrigerator.

3 Heat the barbecue or electric barbecue grill to high. Place a sheet of baking paper on the grill bars, making a few slashes between the bars for ventilation. Place cutlets on grill and cook for 3 minutes each side for medium and 4 minutes for well-done. When cooked, transfer to a serving plate and top each cutlet with a round slice of Cajun butter.

Teriyaki Tenderloins

1 lb chicken tenderloins

Teriyaki Marinade
1/2 cup soy sauce
2 tbsp brown sugar
1/2 tsp ground ginger
2 tbsp wine vinegar
1 clove garlic, crushed
2 tbsp tomato sauce

1 For marinade, mix all ingredients together.
2 Place tenderloins in a non-metal container and stir in about 1/2 cup Teriyaki marinade. Cover and marinate for 30 minutes at room temperature or place in the refrigerator for several hours or overnight in the refrigerator.
3 Heat the barbecue until hot. Place a sheet of baking paper over the grill bars and make a few slits between the bars for ventilation, or place baking paper on the hot plate. Place the tenderloins on grill and cook for 2 minutes on each side until cooked through and golden. Brush with marinade as they cook.

Serves 2-4
Preparation 5 mins plus marinating time
Cooking 5 mins
Calories 181
Fat <1

Serving Suggestions:
1. Serve with steamed rice and vegetables.
2. Toss into salad greens to make a hot salad. Dress salad with 1 tablespoon teriyaki marinade, 1 tablespoon vinegar and 3 tablespoons salad oil.
3. Stuff into heated pocket breads along with shredded lettuce, cucumber and onion rings, and drizzle with an extra spoonful of teriyaki marinade.

Chicken Patties Served on Basil Flapjacks with Chili Yogurt Sauce

Patties
1 lb ground chicken meat
1/2 tsp salt
1/4 tsp pepper
1 tsp crushed garlic
1/2 tsp fresh chopped chili or chili powder
2 tbsp dried breadcrumbs
1/4 cup water

Flapjacks
1 cup all purpose flour
1/4 tsp baking powder
1/4 tsp salt
2 tbsp chopped basil
1 tsp crushed garlic
3/4 cup milk
1 egg

Chili Yogurt Sauce
1 cup natural yogurt
2 tsp sweet chili sauce or to taste

1 Mix all patty ingredients together and knead a little with one hand to distribute ingredients and make it fine in texture. Cover and rest in refrigerator for 20 minutes. With wet hands, form into small flat patties about 1 inch in diameter. Place on a flat tray until needed and refrigerate.
2 Prepare batter for flapjacks. Sift the flour, baking powder and salt into a bowl. Then mix together with the blended basil and garlic and the milk, then beat in the egg. Make a well in the center of the flour and pour in the milk mixture. Stir to form a smooth batter. Cover and set aside for 20 minutes.
3 Heat barbecue until hot and oil the grill bars and hotplate. Brush the patties with a little oil and place on grill bars. Grill for 2 minutes each side, cook the flapjacks at the same time, pour 1/4 cup of mixture onto the greased hotplate. Cook until bubbles appear over the surface and the bottom is golden. Flip over with an eggslice and cook until golden. Transfer to a clean towel and cover to keep hot.
4 Serve a flapjack on each plate and arrange 3 patties on top.
5 For Chili Yogurt Sauce; mix both ingredients together well and then place a dollop of sauce on top of the patties. Serve with a side salad and the extra flapjacks.

Serves 6
Preparation 30 mins
Cooking 5 mins
Calories 240
Fat 2g

Pork Chops with Chili Rice and Glazed Apples

Serves 4-6
Preparation 5 mins
Cooking 15 mins
Calories 450
Fat 4g

6 pork loin chops $^1/_2$ in thick
salt and pepper
2 large apples, cored and cut into thick rings
2 tsp chili powder
4 cups cooked rice

Soy and Honey Marinade
$^3/_4$ cup soy sauce
6 tbsp honey
3 tbsp sherry
6 cloves garlic, crushed
3 tsp grated fresh ginger

1 For soy and honey marinade, mix all ingredients in a small saucepan and simmer for 2-3 minutes.

2 Trim fat from chops as desired and sprinkle lightly with salt and pepper.

3 Heat barbecue until hot and oil the grill bars. Place the chops on grill and sear one side for one minute, turn and brush with soy and honey marinade to glaze. Continue to turn at 2 minute intervals 4 or 5 times more until cooked to required degree. Take care not to overcook. Cooking time is from 10-15 minutes depending on thickness of chops and type of barbecue used.

4 Place apple rings on the grill bars a little after the chops commence cooking. Turn 2-3 times until soft and glazed. Place a piece of baking paper under the apples to prevent scorching. If cooking on a charcoal barbecue, use foil which has been brushed with oil.

5 Mix the chili and cooked rice together and heat on the side of the barbecue in a foil or metal dish. Serve chops with chili rice and garnish with glazed apple rings.

Hot Dogs with Mustard Relish

12 frankfurters or thin sausages
1 cup barbecue sauce
12 hot dog rolls
mild mustard for serving
gherkin relish or tomato pickles to serve

1 Heat the barbecue and oil the grill bars. Place frankfurters or sausages, turn to heat on the grill evenly, so the skin does not burst. Continue to cook for 10-12 minutes, brushing with a little barbecue sauce as they are turned. Push to cooler part of barbecue if cooking too quickly, or turn down the heat.

2 Split the rolls, keeping the 2 halves attached and place cutside down on hot plate to toast.

3 Fill the roll with frankfurter or sausage, squeeze a row of mustard along the side and spoon in the gherkin relish or tomato pickles.

Serves 12
Preparation 1 min
Cooking 12 mins
Calories 370 each
Fat 9g each

Perfect Sirloin Steak

Serves 4
Preparation 5 mins plus marinating time
Cooking 5-15mins
Calories 344
Fat 10g

4 sirloin steaks
2 tsp crushed garlic
2 tsp oil
salt and pepper

Garlic Butter
4 tbsp butter
1 tsp crushed garlic
1 tbsp parsley flakes
2 tsp lemon juice

1 Bring the steaks to room temperate. Mix garlic, oil, and salt and pepper together. Rub onto both sides of the steak. Stand for 10-15 minutes at room temperature.

2 Heat the barbecue until hot and oil the grill bars. Arrange the steaks and sear for one minute each side. Move steaks to cooler part of the barbecue to continue cooking over moderate heat, or turn heat down. If heat cannot be reduced then elevate on a wire cakerack placed on the grill bars. Cook until desired doneness is achieved. Total time 5-6 minutes for rare, 7-10 minutes for medium and 10-14 minutes for well done. Turn during cooking.

3 Serve on a heated steak plate and top with a dollop of garlic butter. For Garlic Butter, mix all ingredients together and serve in a small pot with a spoon.

Toasted Steak Sandwiches

1 lb topside steak
2 tbsp lemon juice
1 tsp crushed garlic
salt and pepper
1 tbsp oil
butter for spreading
10 slices toasted bread
2 large onions, thinly sliced
1 tbsp oil
steak sauce of choice

1 Cut the topside steak into 4 or 5 pieces and pound with a meat mallet until thin. Place in a non-metal container. Mix the lemon juice, garlic, salt, pepper, and oil together, and pour over the steaks. Turn to coat both sides and marinate for 30 minutes at room temperature, or longer in the refrigerator.

2 Soften the butter and spread a thin coating on both sides of the bread. If desired mix a little garlic into the butter.

3 Heat barbecue until hot and oil the grill bars and hotplate. Place onions on the hotplate. Toss and drizzle with a little oil as they cook. When beginning to soften, push to one side and turn occasionally with tongs. Place toast on hotplate and cook until golden on both sides. Place steaks on grill bars and cook 2 minutes on each side.

4 Assemble sandwiches as food cooks by placing steak and onions on one slice of toast, topping with a good squirt of steak sauce and closing with second slice of toast.

Note: A great favorite for backyard barbecue gatherings or fun family meals. Flat-top barbecues, the hot plate or kettle barbecues are best. May also be cooked on electric barbecue grills. For each sandwich allow approximately 3oz of raw steak per serving.

Serves Yields 5 sandwiches
Preparation 8 mins
Cooking 9 mins
Calories 209 each
Fat 2g each

Quick Sesame Chicken Wings

Note: Serve as finger food.

Serves 24 wings
Preparation 5 mins plus marinating time
Cooking 8 mins
Calories 178 each
Fat 4g each

4lb chicken wings, tips removed
3 tbsp soy and honey marinade
sesame seeds, toasted

Soy and Honey Marinade
$^1/_4$ cup soy sauce
2 tbsp honey
1 tbsp sherry
2 cloves garlic, crushed
1 tsp grated fresh ginger

1 To make Soy & Honey Marinade: mix all ingredients together well.
2 Place wings in a large container and smother with the marinade. Cover and marinate for 30 minutes at room temperature or longer in the refrigerator.
3 Place half the wings in a microwave-safe dish and microwave for 10 minutes on high. Remove and microwave the remainder.
4 Heat the barbecue until hot. Place a wire cake-rack over the grill bars and place the wings on the rack. Brush with marinade left in the bowl. Turn and brush the wings frequently until they are brown and crisp.
5 Spread sesame seeds on a foil tray and place on the barbecue. Shake occasionally as they toast. Sprinkle over the browned chicken wings.

Lamb and Salsa Pockets

1/2 leg of lamb
1 tbsp lemon juice
salt and pepper
2 tsp oil
1 tsp crushed garlic
bamboo skewers, soaked
1 1/4 cups tomato salsa
6 pack pocket bread
3 cups shredded lettuce

1 Cut lamb into 1/2 in cubes. Place in a bowl and add lemon juice, salt, pepper, oil and garlic. Cover and marinate at room temperature for 20 minutes. Thread onto skewers.

2 Heat the barbecue and oil the grill bars. Place the salsa into a foil or metal container and place at side of barbecue to heat a little.

3 Cook lamb skewers for 3-4 minutes each side. Halve the pocket bread and heat a little on the barbecue. Open the pocket, fill with lettuce, lamb (skewer removed), and top with heated salsa.Serve immediately.

Serves 6
Preparation 10 mins plus marinating time
Cooking 8 mins
Calories 380
Fat 4g

Fish and Shellfish

Many people may think that seafood is out of the question if they are pressed for time, but our expert team has worked hard to ensure that you can enjoy this little luxury without spending hours in the kitchen. Take a bite into our Honey and Chili Shrimp, make a meal of our Monkfish and Parma Ham, or feast on our Seared Salmon with Rosemary Sweet Potatoes, and you will never order take-out again! Whether for an individual meal or for hosting guests, keep these recipes handy because we know you will revisit them time and time again.

Potato Gnocchi and Pesto Mussels

Serves 3-4
Preparation 5 mins
Cooking 10 mins
Calories 810
Fat 13g

10 oz potato and semolina gnocchi (or other type)
4 tbsp olive oil
1 onion finely chopped
1 lb black mussels, cleaned
1/2 cup dry white wine
3 vine ripened tomatoes, diced
1/2 cup grated Parmesan

Pesto
1 handfull of basil leaves
1 handfull of flat parsley leaves
1/2 cup virgin olive oil
1/2 cup grated Parmesan
6 garlic cloves, crushed
salt and pepper
1 tbsp pine nuts

1 To prepare pesto, blend all ingredients together until they reach a smooth paste consistency.
2 Cook gnocchi in boiling water for around 5 minutes.
3 While gnocchi are cooking, place oil in a large pot on medium heat and add onion. Cook for 1 minute.
4 Add mussels and white wine and cook with lid on. Add tomatoes.
5 When mussels are cooked (about 5 minutes), add gnocchi, tomato mixture, and pesto. Mix well.
6 Serve hot with grated Parmesan.

Monkfish and Parma Ham with Braised Peppers

3 tbsp extra virgin olive oil
4 large bell peppers red, green, orange, or yellow, deseeded and thickly sliced
4 cloves garlic, chopped
2 sprigs fresh thyme
salt and black pepper
4 monkfish fillets, about 1/2 lb each
4 slices Parma ham
2 tbsp balsamic vinegar
chopped fresh basil to garnish

1 Heat 2 tablespoons of the oil in a large heavy-based saucepan, then add the peppers, garlic, thyme, 2 tablespoons of water, and seasoning. Cook, partially covered, for 20 minutes or until softened and browned, stirring occasionally.

2 Meanwhile, season the monkfish well, then wrap a slice of Parma ham around each fillet. Secure the ham with a wetted cocktail stick. Heat the remaining oil in a large heavy-based frying pan, add the fillets and fry for 8-10 minutes, turning once, until browned and cooked through. Cover loosely with foil and set aside.

3 Add the balsamic vinegar to the peppers in the pan and cook for 5 minutes to warm through. Remove the cocktail sticks, then cut the monkfish into thick slices and garnish with the fresh basil. Serve with the peppers and any pan juices.

Note: Delicately flavored monkfish wrapped in Parma ham is a wonderfully luxurious combination. For a really pretty dish, make sure you choose different-colored peppers.

Serves 4
Preparation 10 mins
Cooking 25 mins
Calories 303
Fat 4g

Seared Salmon with Rosemary Sweet Potatoes

OVEN TEMPERATURE
450°F, 230°C, GAS 8

Note: Garlic and rosemary-infused sweet potatoes served with salmon fillets make an inspired partnership. A drizzle of oil and a squeeze of lemon round things off perfectly.

Serves 4
Preparation 15 mins
Cooking 25 mins
Calories 616
Fat 8g

1½ lb sweet potatoes, cut into ½ inch dice
2 cloves garlic, roughly chopped
1 tbsp chopped fresh rosemary, plus sprigs to garnish
3 tbsp olive oil
1 tbsp black peppercorns
4 salmon fillets, about 6 oz each
salt and black pepper
olive oil and lemon wedges to serve
fresh rosemary to garnish

1 Preheat the oven. Toss the sweet potatoes with the garlic, rosemary, and 2 tablespoons of the oil. Transfer to a small roasting pan and cook for 20 minutes, stirring halfway through, until softened. Crush the peppercorns using a pestle and mortar. Brush the salmon fillets with the remaining oil, coat with the crushed peppercorns, and season.

2 Heat a ridged cast-iron grill pan or heavy-based frying pan. Add the salmon fillets, skin-side down, and cook for 4 minutes, then turn and cook for a further 1 minute, until cooked through. Cover with foil and set aside.

3 Spoon the potatoes and any pan juices onto plates and top with the salmon fillets. Drizzle over a little olive oil, and serve garnished with lemon wedges and rosemary.

Fresh Crab Tagliatelle

$^3/_4$ lb dried tagliatelle
3 tbsp olive oil
2 cloves garlic, chopped
1 red chili, deseeded and chopped
finely grated rind of 1 lemon
2 fresh dressed crabs, to give about $^3/_4$ lb crabmeat
1 cup single cream
1 tbsp lemon juice
salt and black pepper
2 tbsp chopped fresh parsley to garnish

1 Cook the pasta according to the instructions on the packet, until tender but still firm to the bite, then drain.

2 Meanwhile, heat the oil in a large heavy-based frying pan and gently fry the garlic, chili, and lemon rind for 3-4 minutes, until softened but not browned. Add the crabmeat, cream, and lemon juice and simmer for 1-2 minutes to heat through. Season to taste.

3 Transfer the pasta to serving bowls. Spoon the crab mixture over the top and sprinkle with the parsley to garnish.

Note: This recipe really makes the most of fresh crab's fantastic flavor. By using ready-dressed crabs, you take all the hard work out of making this exotic pasta dish.

Serves 4
Preparation 10 mins
Cooking 15 mins
Calories 525
Fat 7g

Shellfish and Rocket Pizzas

OVEN TEMPERATURE
425°F, 220°C, GAS 7

Note: Anyone who likes good food will love this shellfish and rocket pizza. Halve the quantities if you're cooking for two, and reduce the cooking time by a couple of minutes.

Serves 4
Preparation 10 mins
Cooking 12 mins
Calories 635
Fat 8g

24 whole raw peeled tiger shrimp, defrosted if frozen
2 tbsp olive oil
2 cloves garlic, crushed
12 small prepared squid tubes, cut into rings
2 9-in pizza bases
2 tbsp sun-dried tomato purée
16 anchovy fillets in oil, drained and chopped
1 3/4 cups mozzarella, grated
1/2 cup rocket
Parmesan to serve (optional)

1 Preheat the oven. Put 2 large baking sheets into the oven to heat.

2 Rinse the shrimp, and pat dry with kitchen towels. Heat the oil in a large heavy-based frying pan, add the garlic, shrimp, and squid and stir-fry for 3 minutes, or until the shrimp turn pink and the squid is opaque.

3 Spread the pizza bases with the tomato purée and top with the cooked seafood, anchovies, and mozzarella. Place on the heated baking sheets and cook for 10-12 minutes, until the cheese is golden, swapping shelves halfway through. Scatter the rocket over the pizzas and shave over the Parmesan, if using, with a vegetable peeler.

Spaghetti Vongole

10 oz spaghetti
3 tbsp virgin olive oil
1 onion, chopped very finely
2 garlic cloves, finely chopped
1 lb Vongoles (clams) cleaned and sandless
1/2 cup white wine
salt and pepper
1 tbsp fresh chopped oregano

1 Pre-cook spaghetti in boiling water, refresh in cold water, stir with half the oil and set aside.
2 Heat the remaining oil in a large cooking pot over high heat. Add the onion, garlic, and cook for one minute.
3 Add vongoles, white wine, salt, and pepper.
4 When all vongoles have opened, add spaghetti and oregano, cook for another 2 minutes and serve.

Serves 3-4
Preparation 10 mins
Cooking 25 mins
Calories 460
Fat 2g

Honey and Chili Shrimp

Serves 3-4
Preparation 10 mins
Cooking 10 mins
Calories 213
Fat <1g

1 lb green king shrimp
soaked bamboo skewers

Honey and Chili Marinade
1/4 cup red wine
3/8 cup honey
1/4 tsp ground chili
1 tsp mustard powder

1 To make marinade, mix all ingredients together.
2 Shell the shrimp, leaving on the tails and de-vein. Place in a glass dish and add enough honey and chili marinade to coat well. Cover and marinate in refrigerator for 1 hour. Thread the shrimp onto skewers, either through the side or through the length.
3 Heat the barbecue to medium-high. Place a sheet of baking paper over the grill bars and place the shrimp on the paper. Cook for 4-5 minutes each side: they will turn pink when cooked. Brush with marinade while cooking. Transfer to a platter. Remove skewers and serve immediately.

Swordfish with Cilantro Butter

1/2 cup unsalted butter
2 tbsp finely chopped cilantro
1 tbsp grated Parmesan cheese
4 swordfish steaks
1 tbsp olive oil
4 zucchini, cut into long slices
1 red bell pepper, quartered

1 Cream the butter until soft, and mix in the cilantro and Parmesan. Pile into butter pot and set aside.

2 Heat barbecue grill until hot and brush with oil. Brush fish steaks with oil, place on grill bars and cook 3-4 minutes each side according to thickness. Brush or spray vegetables with oil and place on grill, cook a few minutes on each side. Remove fish steaks and vegetables to heated plates. Top swordfish steak with a generous dollop of cilantro butter mixture and serve immediately.

Serves 4
Preparation 6 mins
Cooking 10 mins
Calories 423
Fat 16g

Salmon with Pineapple Salsa

Serves 4
Preparation 6 mins
Cooking 10 mins
Calories 344
Fat 3g

4 salmon cutlets

Pineapple Salsa
1 cup canned crushed pineapple, drained
2 spring onions, chopped
1 fresh red chili, chopped
1 tbsp lemon juice
2 tbsp chopped fresh mint

1 Cook salmon on a lightly oiled preheated barbecue or under a grill for 3-5 minutes each side or until cooked.

2 Salsa: Combine all ingredients. Serve with salmon.

Seafood and Noodle Stirfry

2 tbsp sesame oil
1 clove garlic, crushed
2 small red chilies, chopped
1 tbsp grated fresh ginger
2 lb prepared mixed seafood
1/2 red bell pepper, sliced
1/2 cup snowpeas, cut into 1 inch pieces
1/2 lb asparagus spears, cut into 1 inch pieces
1 tbsp shredded fresh basil
3/4 lb egg noodles, cooked
1 tbsp cornstarch
1/4 cup hoisin sauce
1/2 cup water
2 tbsp sesame seeds, toasted

1 Heat oil in a wok. Add garlic, chili, and ginger. Stir-fry for 1 minute. Add seafood, red bell pepper, snowpeas, asparagus, and basil. Stir-fry until seafood is just cooked. Add noodles. Stir-fry for 1-2 minutes.

2 Combine cornstarch, hoisin sauce, and water. Stir into pan. Cook, stirring until sauce boils and thickens. Sprinkle with sesame seeds.

Serves 4
Preparation 20 mins
Cooking 5 mins
Calories 464
Fat 3g

Vegetable Dishes

Depart from the dull with a refreshing range of recipes that get the most out of everyday vegetables. While every family has its favorites, from the humble baked potato to buttered beans, it is comforting to know that you can tempt the tastebuds with a variety of new ideas. Try your hand at our Feta and Ricotta Stuffed Tomatoes or our Creamy Polenta, Spinach, and Cheese Bake, because they are delicious, nutritious and simple to prepare. A trip to your green grocer will open up a whole new world of possibilities. If only everything in life was this easy…

Asparagus, Ricotta, and Herb Frittata

Note: Grilling the asparagus brings extra texture and flavor to this Italian-style omelette - and the creamy ricotta adds the finishing touch. Serve with warmed crusty ciabatta.

Serves 4
Preparation 10 mins
Cooking 20 mins
Calories 430
Fat 8g

1 lb fresh asparagus
12 medium eggs
2 small cloves garlic, crushed
4 tbsp chopped fresh mixed herbs, to include basil, chives and parsley
salt and black pepper
4 tbsp butter
3/8 cup ricotta
squeeze of lemon juice
olive oil or truffle oil to drizzle
Parmesan to serve and fresh chives to garnish

1 Preheat the grill to high. Place the asparagus in a grill pan and grill for 10 minutes or until charred and tender, turning once. Keep warm.
2 Meanwhile, whisk together the eggs, garlic, herbs, and seasoning. Melt 2 tablespoons of the butter in an ovenproof frying pan until it starts to foam, then immediately pour in a quarter of the egg mixture and cook for 1-2 minutes, stirring occasionally, until almost set.
3 Place under the preheated grill for 3-4 minutes, until the egg is cooked through and the top of the frittata is set, then transfer to a plate. Keep warm while you make the 3 remaining frittatas, adding more butter when necessary.
4 Arrange a quarter of the asparagus and a quarter of the ricotta over each frittata, squeeze over the lemon juice, season and drizzle with oil. Top with shavings of Parmesan and garnish with fresh chives.

Pesto Pasta

1 lb fettuccine or other pasta of your choice

Basil and Garlic Pesto
1 large bunch fresh basil
1/2 bunch fresh parsley, broken into sprigs
1/2 cup grated Parmesan or Romano cheese
1/4 cup pine nuts or almonds
2 large cloves garlic, quartered
freshly ground black pepper
1/3 cup olive oil

1 To make pesto, place basil leaves, parsley, Parmesan or Romano cheese, pine nuts or almonds, garlic, and black pepper to taste in a food processor or blender and process to finely chop. With machine running, slowly add oil and continue processing to make a smooth paste.

2 Cook pasta in boiling water in a large saucepan, following packet directions. Drain and divide between serving bowls, top with pesto, toss to combine, and serve immediately.

Note: Spinach pesto makes a tasty alternative when fresh basil is unavailable. To make, use fresh spinach in place of the basil and add 1 teaspoon dried basil.

Serves 4
Preparation 8 mins
Cooking 15 mins
Calories 797
Fat 7g

Roman Kebabs

Oven temperature
450°F, 230°C, Gas 8

Note: Grilling the asparagus brings extra texture and flavor to this Italian-style omelette –and the creamy ricotta adds the finishing touch. Serve with warmed crusty ciabatta.

Serves 4
Preparation 10 mins
Cooking 8 mins
Calories 597
Fat 10g

wooden skewers
1 French bread baton
1 lb mozzarella
4 tomatoes
5 tbsp olive oil
1 tbsp lemon juice
1 tsp dried oregano
salt and black pepper
fresh basil to garnish

1 Preheat the oven. Soak four wooden skewers in water for 10 minutes.

2 Cut bread into 16 ½ inch-thick slices, and then cut the mozzarella into 12 slices. Slice each tomato into 3, discarding the ends.

3 Combine the oil, lemon juice, oregano, and seasoning in a shallow dish. Generously brush both sides of the bread with the oil, then thread the bread onto the skewers, alternating with the mozzarella and tomato slices and finishing with bread. Pour over any of the remaining oil mixture.

4 Place the kebabs on a baking sheet and cook for 6-8 minutes, carefully turning over halfway through, until the bread is crisp and the cheese just starting to melt. Cool slightly before serving garnished with the fresh basil.

Creamy Polenta, Spinach, and Cheese Bake

1 tbsp olive oil
1 small onion, finely chopped
2 cloves garlic, crushed
1/2 tsp ground cilantro
1 lb fresh spinach
1 1/4 cups single cream
1/2 cup Gorgonzola, crumbled
pinch of ground nutmeg
salt and black pepper
1 lb ready-made polenta, thinly sliced
1 mozzarella ball (about 5 oz), thinly sliced

1 Preheat the oven. Heat the oil in a saucepan and gently fry onion, garlic and cilantro for 5 minutes, or until the onion is softened.

2 Blanch the spinach in boiling salted water for one minute, refresh under cold running water, then drain well and squeeze out any excess moisture. Stir the spinach into the pan with the cream, Gorgonzola, nutmeg, salt, and pepper. Bring to a simmer, then transfer to a large, shallow, ovenproof dish.

3 Arrange the polenta and mozzarella slices over the top of the spinach mixture, pressing down well. Bake for 15 minutes or until bubbling. Preheat the grill to high. Place the bake under the grill for 1-2 minutes, until browned.

OVEN TEMPERATURE
450°F, 230°C, GAS 8

Note: Bubbling mozzarella covers ready-made polenta and a bed of creamy spinach to make this great-tasting vegetarian supper dish. Serve it with a green salad.

Serves 4
Preparation 10 mins
Cooking 25 mins
Calories 463
Fat 8g

Spinach, Olive, and Feta Frittata

Serves 4
Preparation 15 mins
Cooking 25 mins
Calories 616
Fat 8g

10 eggs
1 tbsp oregano, fresh, chopped
black pepper, freshly crushed
5 tbsp olive oil
1/2 lb potatoes, peeled and diced
1 brown onion, diced
1 clove garlic, crushed
2 cups baby spinach
4 tbsp pitted kalamata olives, halved
1/2 cup feta, crumbled
1/2 cup semi-dried tomatoes
3 large red bell peppers

1 Combine the eggs and oregano in a bowl, and season with black pepper. Set aside.
2 Heat the oil in a 9 inch pan and sauté the potato, onion, and garlic for a few minutes (until soft).
3 Add the spinach and cook (until spinach begins to wilt). Remove the pan from the heat, then add olives, feta, and semi-dried tomatoes.
4 Return the pan to a very low heat, pour in the egg mixture, and cook for 10-15 minutes. Run a spatula around the sides of the pan as the frittata is cooking, and tilt it slightly while cooking (so that egg mixture runs down the sides a little).
5 When frittata is almost done through the middle, place under a grill for five minutes to cook and brown the top.
6 Serve in wedges with the roasted pepper sauce.
7 *For the sauce:* Halve the bell peppers and remove the seeds. Chargrill the bell peppers until black. Let them cool, and remove the skins. Place into a food processor and process until puréed. Transfer to a bowl. Makes 1 cup.

Feta and Ricotta Stuffed Tomatoes

6 large firm tomatoes
1 cup feta cheese, crumbed
1 cup ricotta cheese
4 tbsp pine nuts, chopped
10 black olives, stoned and chopped
1$^1/_2$ tbsp fresh oregano, chopped
3 tbsp wholemeal breadcrumbs
freshly ground black pepper
6 black olives, to garnish
oregano leaves

1 Preheat oven. Cut the top quarters off each tomato, and scoop the centers into a bowl. Dice the tops, and add to the bowl. Combine half the tomato mixture with the feta, ricotta, pine nuts, olives, oregano, breadcrumbs, and pepper. Beat mixture together, and spoon back into the cases (piling the tops high).

3 Place in a shallow oven-proof dish and bake for 20-25 minutes.

4 Garnish with an olive and oregano to serve.

OVEN TEMPERATURE
180°C, 350°F, GAS MARK 4

Serves 6
Preparation 8 mins
Cooking 25 mins
Calories 198
Fat 6g

Deep-Fried Okra

Serves 4
Preparation 8 mins
Cooking 2 mins
Calories 283
Fat 2g

Note: The garlic walnut sauce goes very well with chicken, fish, or vegetables.

1/2 lb okra
1 egg
1 cup flour
1 cup ice cold water
oil, for frying

Garlic Walnut Sauce
2 slices bread
1/2 cup water
1/2 cup walnuts
2 cloves garlic, roughly chopped
2 tbsp white wine vinegar
1 tbsp olive oil
salt and pepper to taste

1 Wash and trim okra. In a large bowl, whisk egg until frothy, add flour and water, and whisk together (until batter is also frothy).
2 Heat the oil in a large frying pan, dip okra in batter, cook in oil for 1-2 minutes (or until lightly brown).
3 Drain on absorbent paper, serve with lemon wedges and garlic walnut sauce.

Garlic Walnut Sauce
In a small bowl, soak bread in water for 5 minutes. Squeeze out the water Place walnuts in food processor, and process until finely chopped. Add bread, garlic, and white wine vinegar. Process until combined. While motor is running, add olive oil, salt and pepper, process until a paste is formed.

Eggplant Rolls

2 eggplant (about 1/2 lb each)
3 tbsp olive oil
3 medium tomatoes, seeded and diced
1 cup mozzarella cheese, finely diced
2 tbsp fresh basil, chopped
salt and freshly ground black pepper
fresh basil leaves, for serving

Dressing
4 tbsp olive oil
1 tomato, diced
1 tbsp balsamic vinegar
2 tbsp pine nuts, toasted

1 Remove the stalks from eggplant and slice the eggplant lengthwise thinly 2 in. Brush the slices on both sides with oil, and grill on both sides (until soft and beginning to brown).
2 Preheat the oven. Combine together (in a bowl) the tomatoes, mozzarella, basil, and seasoning. Spoon a little onto the end of each slice of eggplant, and roll up. Place seam-side down in a greased oven-proof dish, bake for 15-17 minutes.
3 In a small pan, using a little of the dressing oil, sauté the tomato until softened. Add the remaining oil, balsamic vinegar, and pine nuts, and gently warm. Season to taste. Arrange the rolls on a platter, and spoon the dressing over the rolls.
4 Garnish with fresh basil leaves to serve.

OVEN TEMPERATURE
350°F, 180°C, GAS MARK 4

Serves 4
Preparation 8 mins
Cooking 8 mins
Calories 384
Fat 7g

Asparagus and Lemon Risotto

Note: Rich, creamy, and full of flavor, this is a fabulous risotto and it's really easy to make. Be sure not to overcook it, each grain of rice should keep its shape and firmness.

Serves 6
Preparation 15 mins
Cooking 25 mins
Calories 363
Fat 3g

2 tbsp olive oil
1 onion, chopped
2 cups arborio rice
1 cup white wine
3 cups chicken or vegetable stock
1 cup asparagus tips, cut into bite-sized pieces
4 tbsp butter
1/2 cup Parmesan, grated
salt and black pepper
2 tbsp chopped fresh parsley
finely grated rind of 1 lemon

1 Heat the oil in a large, heavy-based saucepan or frying pan, then add the onion and fry for 3-4 minutes, until golden. Add the rice and stir for 1 minute or until coated with the oil. Stir in the wine and bring to the boil, then reduce the heat and continue stirring for 4-5 minutes, until the wine has been absorbed by the rice.

2 Pour about one-third of the stock into the rice and simmer for 4-5 minutes, until the stock has been absorbed, stirring constantly. Add half the remaining stock and cook, stirring, until absorbed. Add the remaining stock and the asparagus and cook, stirring, for 5 minutes or until the rice and asparagus are tender but still firm to the bite.

3 Add the butter and half the Parmesan and season. Cook for 1 minute, or until the butter and cheese have melted into the rice, stirring constantly. Sprinkle with the remaining Parmesan the parsley and lemon rind.

Pumpkin with Lemon and Cheese

$1^1/_2$ lb pumpkin or squash, peeled, seeded and cut into chunks
1 cup chicken or vegetable stock
2 tsp arrowroot
grated rind of $^1/_2$ lemon and juice of 1 lemon
1 cup mature Cheddar, grated
2 tbsp chopped fresh dill or parsley
salt and pepper

1 Place the pumpkin or squash in a steamer or in a metal colander covered with foil. Set over a saucepan of simmering water and steam for 5-10 minutes, until tender but still firm.

2 Meanwhile, bring the stock to the boil in a small saucepan. Mix the arrowroot with the lemon juice until smooth, then stir in the lemon rind and add to the boiling stock. Simmer, stirring constantly, for 1-2 minutes, until sauce thickens and looks glossy. Add $^1/_2$ cup of the Cheddar and simmer for a further 1-2 minutes, until the cheese has melted. Stir in the dill or parsley, season, and mix well.

3 Preheat the grill to high. Transfer the pumpkin to a flameproof dish, pour over the lemon sauce, and sprinkle with the reserved Cheddar. Place under the grill and cook for 5-8 minutes, until the sauce is bubbling and golden.

Serves 6
Preparation 15 mins
Cooking 20 mins
Calories 127
Fat 8g

Desserts and Sweet Things

Take a trip to seventh heaven with our delectable range of dishes. Never before has it been so easy to make up a dessert that is totally satisfying and requiring so little fuss from start to finish. Sink your teeth into our Shaggy Dog Lamingtons, or plunge your fork into our Peach and Hazelnut Crumble, and you will know that the best-loved course on the dinnertime menu need not be just a solitary tub of ice-cream. Not when you have the know-how to prepare desserts and sweet things that will have you and your family begging for more!

Mini Chocolate Muffins with Mocha Sauce

OVEN TEMPERATURE
350°F, 180°C, GAS 4

Note: You'll need a 12-hole, non-stick muffin tray for these mini muffins or, if you prefer, you can make large muffins and increase the cooking time to 25 minutes.

Serves makes 12
Preparation 10 mins plus 5 mins cooling
Cooking 15 mins
Calories 160 each
Fat 11g each

4 tbsp unsalted butter, diced, plus extra for greasing
1/2 cup plain chocolate, broken into pieces
2 medium eggs
1/3 cup superfine sugar
3/4 cup all purpose flour
1/4 tsp baking powder
1/5 cup cocoa powder, sifted, plus extra for dusting

Mocha Sauce
1 cup plain chocolate, broken into pieces
1/3 cup espresso or other strong, good quality coffee
5/8 cup double cream

1 Preheat the oven. Grease a 12-hole muffin tray. Melt the chocolate and butter in a bowl set over a saucepan of simmering water. Put the eggs, sugar, flour, baking powder, and cocoa powder into a bowl and beat for 1 minute, then beat in the melted chocolate and butter.

2 Spoon into the muffin tray, allowing 1 tablespoon for each hole. Bake for 15 minutes or until risen and firm to the touch.

3 Meanwhile, make the mocha sauce. Put the chocolate, coffee and 1/4 cup of cream into a small pan and heat gently. Simmer for 1-2 minutes, until the sauce has thickened slightly. Keep warm.

4 Leave the muffins to cool on a wire rack for 5 minutes. Whisk the remaining cream until thickened, then spoon over the muffins together with the mocha sauce. Serve dusted with cocoa powder.

Raspberry and Elderflower Fool

3 cups raspberries, defrosted if frozen, plus extra to decorate
4 tbsp elderflower cordial
4 tbsp confectioner's sugar, or to taste, plus extra to dust
2 cups double cream
fresh mint to decorate

1 Purée the raspberries and elderflower cordial until smooth in a food processor or with a hand blender. Blend in the confectioners' sugar. Spoon 1 tablespoon of the mixture into each dessert glass, reserving the remaining purée, and set aside.

2 Whisk the cream until it holds its shape, then gradually fold in the reserved raspberry purée.

3 Spoon the raspberry cream into the glasses and chill in the fridge for 30 minutes. Serve decorated with the extra raspberries and mint and dusted with confectioner's sugar.

Note: A fresh-tasting fruit fool that needs no cooking. Other fruits such as strawberries or blackberries can be used, but you may need to adjust the quantity of confectioners' sugar.

Serves 6
Preparation 15 mins
Calories 371
Fat 36g

Extra-light Banana Clafoutis

OVEN TEMPERATURE
450°F, 230°C, GAS 8

Note: Clafoutis is traditionally made with cherries, but using bananas gives the pudding a wonderful richness. It's good served on its own, with double cream or vanilla ice cream.

6 tbsp butter, melted
3 tbsp molasses or soft dark brown sugar
grated rind and juice of 1 lemon
3 tbsp rum
2 lb bananas, cut into chunks
1 cup half-fat milk
4 eggs, separated
3 tbsp sugar
1 cup plain flour
1 tsp ground cinnamon
confectioners' sugar to dust

1 Preheat the oven to 450°F/230°C/Gas Mark 8. Place the melted butter, molasses or sugar, lemon rind, and juice and the rum in a 13 x 9 inch ovenproof dish and mix well. Add the bananas and toss to coat. Cook for 12-15 minutes, basting frequently, until the bananas have softened.

2 Meanwhile, gently warm the milk in a small saucepan. Beat the egg yolks and sugar until pale and creamy. Beat in the warmed milk, then the flour and cinnamon. Whisk the whites until they form soft peaks, then fold gently into the mixture.

3 Remove the bananas from the oven and reduce the temperature to 400°F/200°C/Gas Mark 6. Pour the batter over the bananas and return the dish to the oven. Bake for 20-25 minutes, until browned and well-risen. Check the pudding is cooked by inserting a skewer into the center; it should come out clean. Allow to cool slightly–the mixture will sink rapidly as it cools, then dust with confectioners' sugar and serve warm.

Serves 6
Preparation 15 mins
Cooking 40 mins
Calories 425
Fat 3g

Serves 4 **Preparation** 20 mins plus 15 mins cooling time **Cooking** 8 mins **Calories** 209 **Fat** 2g

Summer Fruit Compote with Vanilla Yogurt

1 1/2 lb mixed summer berries, hulled or stalks removed and defrosted if frozen
1/2 cup port wine
1/3 cup superfine sugar
2 strips orange rind
juice of 1 orange
1 tsp ground mixed spice

Vanilla Yogurt
1 vanilla pod, split
1 cup Greek yogurt
1 tbsp clear honey

1 To make the vanilla yogurt, scrape the seeds from the vanilla pod into the yogurt and stir in the honey. Cover and refrigerate while you make the compote.

2 Put the berries into a saucepan with the port wine, superfine sugar, orange rind, and juice and the mixed spice. Heat for 5-8 minutes, until the fruit is just softened. Remove from the heat and set aside for 15 minutes to cool slightly. Serve the warm compote with a spoonful of vanilla yogurt.

Note: Thick vanilla yogurt made with clear honey has a real Mediterranean flavor, and tastes fabulous with this warm summer fruit compote. Serve with dessert cookies.

Sweet Brioche with Grilled Peaches

Note: Don't worry if the peach stones won't come out easily, simply cut the fruit away from the stone in thick juicy slices and grill them for slightly less time than the halves.

Serves 4
Preparation 10 mins
Cooking 12 mins
Calories 420
Fat 24g

4 large, ripe peaches, halved and stoned
1 tbsp clear honey
6 tbsp unsalted butter
2 medium eggs, lightly beaten
2 tbsp sweet white wine
2 tbsp superfine sugar
1 tbsp lemon juice
pinch of ground cinnamon
4 slices brioche
crème fraîche to serve

1 Preheat the grill to medium. Place the peach halves, cut-side up, in a grill pan and top each one with a drizzle of honey and a knob of butter, reserving half the butter for frying. Grill for 5-6 minutes, until softened and golden.

2 Meanwhile, whisk together the eggs, sweet white wine, sugar, lemon juice, and cinnamon. Dip the slices of brioche in the egg mixture to coat.

3 Melt the remaining butter in a large frying pan and gently fry the brioche slices for 2-3 minutes on each side, until crisp and golden. Top each slice with 2 peach halves and their juices and a spoonful of crème fraîche.

Almond Cakes

3 1/2 cups almonds, blanched
1 cup superfine sugar
2 medium eggs
1/4 cup soft white bread crumbs
3/8 cup liquid honey

1 Grind almonds in a food processor (with a little of the sugar). Combine the remaining sugar with the eggs, and whisk until pale and creamy. Add the ground almonds to the bread crumbs, and stir until well combined.

2 Preheat oven.

3 Shape (using a tablespoon) roughly into diamond shapes, and place on a non-stick baking sheet. Bake for 15 minutes.

4 While warm, place on wire cooling racks, and brush with warm honey. Leave to cool a little before serving.

OVEN TEMPERATURE
350°F, 180°C, GAS 4

Serves 38-40 cakes
Preparation 10 mins
Cooking 15 mins
Calories 114 each
Fat <1 each

Flourless Chocolate Cake

OVEN TEMPERATURE
350°F, 180°C, GAS 4

Serves 12-14
Preparation 10 mins
Cooking 45 mins
Calories 188 each
Fat 6g each serving

6 eggs, separated
1/2 cup superfine sugar
1/5 cup cocoa powder, sifted
1 cup dark chocolate, melted

Toffee
1/2 cup superfine sugar

1 Beat egg yolks with sugar until thick and creamy. Mix in cocoa powder and chocolate. Beat egg whites until soft peaks form. Fold into chocolate mixture. Pour into a greased and lined 9 inch springform pan. Bake for 35 minutes. Cool. Garnish with toffee.
2 Toffee: Melt sugar in a heavy saucepan over high heat. Shake saucepan so that sugar browns evenly. Bring to a boil. Cook until golden. Pour onto a sheet of greased foil. Set. Break into large pieces.

Rum Raisin Nut Brownies

$^1/_2$ cup raisins
$^1/_4$ cup brandy
$^1/_2$ cup dark chocolate, chopped
$^1/_2$ cup unsalted butter
2 eggs
$^7/_8$ cup brown sugar
1 cup flour, sifted
1 cup macadamia or brazil nuts, chopped
superfine sugar, sifted, for dusting
drinking chocolate, sifted, for dusting

1 Place raisins and brandy in a bowl and set aside to soak for 15 minutes or until raisins soften.

2 Place chocolate and butter in a heatproof bowl set over a saucepan of simmering water and heat, stirring constantly, until mixture is smooth. Remove bowl from pan and set aside to cool slightly.

3 Place eggs and brown sugar in a bowl and beat until thick and creamy. Add chocolate mixture, flour, nuts, and raisin mixture and mix to combine.

4 Pour mixture into a greased 8 inch square cake pan and bake for 35 minutes, or until firm. Cool brownies in pan. Then cut into squares and dust with superfine sugar and drinking chocolate.

OVEN TEMPERATURE
350°F, 180°C, GAS 4

Note: For a dinner party dessert, top these irresistibly rich and moist brownies with thick cream, a chocolate sauce or berry coulis and a garnish of fresh fruit.

Serves 16
Preparation 15 mins
Cooking 35 mins
Calories 238 each
Fat 7g each

Shaggy Dog Lamingtons

Note: To make coating the cake easier, place coconut and icing in two shallow dishes or cake pans. Use tongs or two forks to dip the cake in the icing, then place on a wire rack set over a sheet of paper and allow to drain for 2-3 minutes before rolling in the coconut.

1 butter or sponge cake
(about 7 x 11 in)
2 cups shredded coconut
1 tbsp drinking chocolate, sifted

Chocolate Cream Filling
1¼ cups cream (double)
1 cup dark chocolate chopped

Chocolate Icing
2 cups confectioner's sugar
2 tbsp cocoa powder
2 tbsp butter, softened
¼ cup milk

1 Cut cake into 2 inch squares. Split each square horizontally and set aside.

2 To make filling, place cream and chocolate in a heatproof bowl set over a saucepan of simmering water and heat, stirring, until chocolate melts and mixture is smooth. Remove bowl from pan and set aside to cool. Beat filling until light and fluffy.

3 Spread filling over bottom half of cake squares and top with remaining cake squares.

4 To make icing, sift confectioner's sugar and cocoa powder together in a bowl, add butter and mix to combine. Stir in enough milk to make an icing with a smooth coating consistency.

5 Dip cake squares in icing to coat completely. Roll in coconut and dust with drinking chocolate. Refrigerate until ready to serve.

Serves makes 12
Preparation 25 mins
Cooking 45 mins
Calories 456 each
Fat 17g each

Peach and Hazelnut Crumble

3 14-oz cans peach halves in natural juice, drained but reserving 1 cup of juice
3 pieces stem ginger in syrup, drained and finely chopped
1 cup plain flour
1 cup roasted chopped hazelnuts
4 tbsp soft light brown sugar
1 tsp ground cinnamon
1/2 cup butter, cubed

Serves 6
Preparation 10 mins
Cooking 45 mins
Calories 424
Fat 24g

1 Preheat the oven. Arrange the peaches, cut-side up, in a 12 x 10 inch ovenproof dish. Sprinkle with the ginger. Boil the reserved juice in a saucepan for 5 minutes or until reduced by a third. Pour over the peaches.

2 In a large bowl, mix together the flour, hazelnuts, sugar, and cinnamon. Add the butter and rub in with the tips of your fingers until the mixture resembles fine breadcrumbs. Sprinkle over the fruit and bake for 30-35 minutes, until browned.

OVEN TEMPERATURE
400°F, 200°C, GAS 6

Note: Canned peaches are a great standby but if you have the time you can use fresh peaches, peeled, stoned, and sliced. Serve this nutty crumble with custard or fresh cream.

Glossary

acidulated water: water with added acid, such as lemon juice or vinegar, which prevents discoloration of ingredients, particularly fruit or vegetables. The proportion of acid to water is 1 teaspoon per 300mL.
al dente: Italian cooking term for ingredients that are cooked until tender but still firm to the bite; usually applied to pasta.
americaine: method of serving seafood–usually lobster and monkfish–in a sauce flavored with olive oil, aromatic herbs, tomatoes, white wine, fish stock, brandy, and tarragon.
anglaise: cooking style for simple cooked dishes such as boiled vegetables. Assiette anglaise is a plate of cold cooked meats.
antipasto: Italian for "before the meal," it denotes an assortment of cold meats, vegetables, and cheeses, often marinated, served as an hors d'oeuvre. A typical antipasto might include salami, prosciutto, marinated artichoke hearts, anchovy fillets, olives, tuna fish, and Provolone cheese.
au gratin: food sprinkled with breadcrumbs, often covered with cheese sauce, and browned until a crisp coating forms.
balsamic vinegar: a mild, extremely fragrant, wine-based vinegar made in northern Italy. Traditionally, the vinegar is aged for at least seven years in a series of casks made of various woods.
baste: to moisten food while it is cooking by spooning or brushing on liquid or fat.
baine marie: a saucepan standing in a large pan, which is filled with boiling water to keep liquids at simmering point. A double boiler will do the same job.
beat: to stir thoroughly and vigorously.
beurre manie: equal quantities of butter and flour kneaded together and added a little at a time to thicken a stew or casserole.
bird: see paupiette.
blanc: a cooking liquid made by adding flour and lemon juice to water in order to keep certain vegetables from discoloring as they cook.
blanch: to plunge into boiling water and then, in some cases, into cold water. Fruits and nuts are blanched to remove skin easily.
blanquette: a white stew of lamb, veal, or chicken, bound with egg yolks and cream and accompanied by onion and mushrooms.
blend: to mix thoroughly.
bonne femme: dishes cooked in the traditional French "housewife" style. Chicken and pork bonne femme are garnished with bacon, potatoes, and baby onion; fish bonne femme with mushrooms in a white wine sauce.
bouquet garni: a bunch of herbs, usually consisting of sprigs of parsley, thyme, marjoram, rosemary, a bay leaf, peppercorns, and cloves, tied in muslin and used to flavor stews and casseroles.
braise: to cook whole or large pieces of poultry, game, fish, meat, or vegetables in a small amount of wine, stock, or other liquid in a closed pot. Often the main ingredient is first browned in fat and then cooked in a low oven or very slowly on top of the stove. Braising suits tough meats and older birds and produces a mellow, rich sauce.
broil: the American term for grilling food.
brown: cook in a small amount of fat until brown.
burghul (also bulgur): a type of cracked wheat, where the kernels are steamed and dried before being crushed.
buttered: to spread with softened or melted butter.
butterfly: to slit a piece of food in half horizontally, cutting it almost through so that when opened it resembles butterfly wings. Chops, large shrimp (prawns), and thick fish fillets are often butterflied so that they cook more quickly.
buttermilk: a tangy, low-fat cultured milk product whose slight acidity makes it an ideal marinade base for poultry.
calzone: a semicircular pocket of pizza dough, stuffed with meat or vegetables, sealed and baked.
caramelize: to melt sugar until it is a golden brown syrup.
champignons: small mushrooms, usually canned.
chasseur: (hunter) a French cooking style in which meat and chicken dishes are cooked with mushrooms, shallots, white wine, and often tomato.
clarify: to melt butter and drain the oil off the sediment.
coat: to cover with a thin layer of flour, sugar, nuts, crumbs, poppy or sesame seeds, cinnamon sugar, or a few of the ground spices.
concasser: to chop coarsely, usually tomatoes.
confit: from the French verb confire, meaning to preserve. Food that is made into a preserve by cooking very slowly and thoroughly until tender. In the case of meat, such as duck or goose, it is cooked in its own fat, and covered with it so that it does not come into contact with the air. Vegetables such as onions are good in confit.
consomme: a clear soup usually made from beef.
coulis: a thin puree, usually of fresh or cooked fruit or vegetables, which is soft enough to pour (couler means "to run"). A coulis may be rough-textured or very smooth.
court bouillon: the liquid in which fish, poultry, or meat is cooked. It usually consists of water with bay leaf, onion, carrots, and salt and freshly ground black pepper to taste. Other additives can include wine, vinegar, stock, garlic, or spring onions (scallions).
couscous: cereal processed from semolina into pellets, traditionally steamed and served with meat and vegetables in the classic North African stew of the same name.
cruciferous vegetables: certain members of the mustard, cabbage, and turnip families with cross-shaped flowers and strong aromas and flavors.
cream: to make soft, smooth, and creamy by rubbing with back of spoon or by beating with mixer. Usually applied to fat and sugar.
croutons: small toasted or fried cubes of bread.
crudites: raw vegetables, whether cut in slices or sticks to nibble plain or with a dipping sauce, or shredded and tossed as salad with a simple dressing.
cube: to cut into small pieces with six equal sides.
curdle: to cause milk or sauce to separate into solid and liquid. Example, overcooked egg mixtures.
daikon radish: (also called mooli) a long white Japanese radish.
Dark sesame oil: (also called Oriental sesame oil) dark polyunsaturated oil with a low burning point, used for seasoning. Do not replace with lighter sesame oil.
deglaze: to dissolve congealed cooking juices or glaze on the bottom of a pan by adding a liquid, then scraping and stirring vigorously while bringing the liquid to the boil. Juices may be used to make gravy or to add to sauce.
degrease: to skim grease from the surface of liquid. If possible the liquid should be chilled so the fat solidifies. If not, skim off most of the fat with a large metal spoon, then trail strips of paper towel on the surface of the liquid to remove any remaining globules.
devilled: a dish or sauce that is highly seasoned with a hot ingredient such as mustard, Worcestershire sauce or cayenne pepper.
dice: to cut into small cubes.
dietary fiber: a plant-cell material that is undigested or only partially digested in the human body, but which promotes healthy digestion of other food matter.
dissolve: mix a dry ingredient with liquid until absorbed.
dredge: to coat with a dry ingredient, as flour or sugar.
drizzle: to pour in a fine thread-like stream over a surface.
dust: to sprinkle or coat lightly with flour or icing sugar.
Dutch oven: a heavy casserole with a lid usually made from cast iron or pottery.
emulsion: a mixture of two liquids that are not mutually soluble– for example, oil and water.
entree: in Europe, the "entry" or hors d'oeuvre; in North America entree means the main course.
fillet: special cut of beef, lamb, pork, or veal; breast of poultry and game; fish cut of the bone lengthways.
flake: to break into small pieces with a fork.
flame: to ignite warmed alcohol over food.
fold in: a gentle, careful combining of a light or delicate mixture with a heavier mixture using a metal spoon.
fricassee: a dish in which poultry, fish, or vegetables are bound together with a white or veloute sauce. In Britain and the United States, the name applies to an old-fashioned dish of chicken in a creamy sauce.
galette: sweet or savoury mixture shaped as a flat round.
garnish: to decorate food, usually with something edible.
gastrique: caramelized sugar deglazed with vinegar and used in fruit-flavored savoury sauces, in such dishes as duck with orange.
glaze: a thin coating of beaten egg, syrup, or aspic which is brushed over pastry, fruits, or cooked meats.
gluten: a protein in flour that is developed when dough is kneaded, making it elastic.

gratin: a dish cooked in the oven or under the grill so that it develops a brown crust. Breadcrumbs or cheese may be sprinkled on top first. Shallow gratin dishes ensure a maximum area of crust.
grease: to rub or brush lightly with oil or fat.
joint: to cut poultry, game, or small animals into serving pieces by dividing at the joint.
julienne: to cut food into match-like strips.
knead: to work dough using heel of hand with a pressing motion, while stretching and folding the dough.
line: to cover the inside of a container with paper, to protect or aid in removing mixture.
infuse: to immerse herbs, spices, or other flavorings in hot liquid to flavor it. Infusion takes from two to five minutes, depending on the flavoring. The liquid should be very hot but not boiling.
jardiniere: a garnish of garden vegetables, typically carrots, pickling onions, French beans, and turnips.
lights: lungs of an animal, used in various meat preparations such as pâtes and faggots.
macerate: to soak food in liquid to soften.
marinade: a seasoned liquid, usually an oil and acid mixture, in which meats or other foods are soaked to soften and give more flavor.
marinara: Italian "sailor's style" cooking that does not apply to any particular combination of ingredients. Marinara tomato sauce for pasta is most familiar.
marinate: to let food stand in a marinade to season and tenderize.
mask: to cover cooked food with sauce.
melt: to heat until liquified.
mince: to grind into very small pieces.
mix: to combine ingredients by stirring.
monounsaturated fats: one of three types of fats found in foods. Are believed not to raise the level of cholesterol in the blood.
nicoise: a garnish of tomatoes, garlic, and black olives; a salad with anchovy, tuna and French beans is typical.
non-reactive pan: a cooking pan whose surface does not chemically react with food. Materials used include stainless steel, enamel, glass, and some alloys.
noisette: small "nut" of lamb cut from boned loin or rack that is rolled, tied, and cut in neat slices. Noisette also means flavored with hazelnuts, or butter cooked to a nut brown colour.
normande: a cooking style for fish, with a garnish of shrimp, mussels, and mushrooms in a white wine cream sauce; for poultry and meat, a sauce with cream, Calvados, and apple.
olive oil: various grades of oil extract from olives. Extra virgin olive oil has a full, fruity flavor and the lowest acidity. Virgin olive oil is slightly higher in acidity and lighter in flavor. Pure olive oil is a processed blend of olive oils and has the highest acidity and lightest taste.
panade: a mixture for binding stuffings and dumplings, notably quenelles, often of choux pastry or simply breadcrumbs. A panade may also be made of frangipane, pureed potatoes, or rice.
papillote: to cook food in oiled or buttered greasepoof paper or aluminium foil. Also a decorative frill to cover bone ends of chops and poultry drumsticks.
parboil: to boil or simmer until part cooked (i.e. cooked further than when blanching).
pare: to cut away outside covering.
pâte: a paste of meat or seafood used as a spread for toast or crackers.
paupiette: a thin slice of meat, poultry, or fish spread with a savoury stuffing and rolled. In the United States this is also called "bird" and in Britain an "olive."
peel: to strip away outside covering.
plump: to soak in liquid or moisten thoroughly until full and round.
poach: to simmer gently in enough hot liquid to cover, using care to retain shape of food.
polyunsaturated fat: one of the three types of fats found in food. These exist in large quantities in such vegetable oils as safflower, sunflower, corn, and soya bean. These fats lower the level of cholesterol in the blood.
puree: a smooth paste, usually of vegetables or fruits, made by putting foods through a sieve, food mill, or liquefying in a blender or food processor.
ragout: traditionally a well-seasoned, rich stew containing meat, vegetables, and wine. Nowadays, a term applied to any stewed mixture.
ramekins: small oval or round individual baking dishes.
reconstitute: to put moisture back into dehydrated foods by soaking in liquid.
reduce: to cook over a very high heat, uncovered, until the liquid is reduced by evaporation.
refresh: to cool hot food quickly, either under running water or by plunging it into iced water, to stop it cooking. Particularly for vegetables, and occasionally for shellfish.
rice vinegar: mild, fragrant vinegar that is less sweet than cider vinegar and not as harsh as distilled malt vinegar. Japanese rice vinegar is milder than the Chinese variety.
roulade: a piece of meat, usually pork or veal, that is spread with stuffing, rolled, and often braised or poached. A roulade may also be a sweet or savoury mixture that is baked in a Swiss roll tin or paper case, filled with a contrasting filling, and rolled.
rubbing-in: a method of incorporating fat into flour, by use of fingertips only. Also incorporates air into mixture.
safflower oil: the vegetable oil that contains the highest proportion of polyunsaturated fats.
salsa: a juice derived from the main ingredient being cooked or a sauce added to a dish to enhance its flavor. In Italy the term is often used for pasta sauces; in Mexico the name usually applies to uncooked sauces served as an accompaniment, especially to corn chips.
saturated fats: one of the three types of fats found in foods. These exist in large quantities in animal products, coconut, and palm oils; they raise the level of cholesterol in the blood. As high cholesterol levels may cause heart disease, saturated fat consumption is recommended to be less than 15% of calories provided by the daily diet.
sauté: to cook or brown in small amount of hot fat.
score: to mark food with cuts, notches of lines to prevent curling or to make food more attractive.
scald: to bring just to boiling point, usually for milk. Also to rinse with boiling water.
sear: to brown surface quickly over high heat in hot dish.
seasoned flour: flour with salt and pepper added.
sift: to shake a dry, powdered substance through a sieve or sifter to remove any lumps and give lightness.
simmer: to cook food gently in liquid that bubbles steadily just below boiling point so that the food cooks in even heat without breaking up.
singe: to quickly flame poultry to remove all traces of feathers after plucking.
skim: to remove a surface layer (often of impurities and scum) from a liquid with a metal spoon or small ladle.
slivered: sliced in long, thin pieces, usually refers to nuts, especially almonds.
soften: ie: gelatine. Sprinkle over cold water and allow to gel (soften) then dissolve and liquefy.
souse: to cover food, particularly fish, in wine vinegar and spices and cook slowly; the food is cooled in the same liquid. Sousing gives food a pickled flavor.
steep: to soak in warm or cold liquid in order to soften food and draw out strong flavors or impurities.
stir-fry: to cook thin slices of meat and vegetable over a high heat in a small amount of oil, stirring constantly to even cooking in a short time. Traditionally cooked in a wok, however a heavy based frying pan may be used.
stock: a liquid containing flavors, extracts, and nutrients of bones, meat, fish, or vegetables.
stud: to adorn with; for example, baked ham studded with whole cloves.
sugo: an Italian sauce made from the liquid or juice extracted from fruit or meat during cooking.
sweat: to cook sliced or chopped food, usually vegetables, in a little fat and no liquid over very low heat. Foil is pressed on top so that the food steams in its own juices, usually before being added to other dishes.
timbale: a creamy mixture of vegetables or meat baked in a mould. French for "kettledrum"; also denotes a drum-shaped baking dish.
thicken: to make a thin, smooth paste by mixing together arrowroot, corn flour, or flour with an equal amount of cold water; stir into hot liquid, cook, stirring until thickened.
toss: to gently mix ingredients with two forks or fork and spoon.
total fat: the individual daily intake of all three fats previously described in this glossary. Nutritionists recommend that fats provide no more than 35% of the energy in the diet.
vine leaves: tender, lightly flavored leaves of the grapevine, used in ethnic cuisine as wrappers for savoury mixtures. As the leaves are usually packed in brine, they should be well rinsed before use.
whip: to beat rapidly, incorporate air, and produce expansion.
zest: thin outer layer of citrus fruits containing the aromatic citrus oil. It is usually thinly pared with a vegetable peeler, or grated with a zester or grater to separate it from the bitter white pith underneath.

Weights & Measures

Cooking is not an exact science: one does not require finely calibrated scales, pipettes, and scientific equipment to cook, yet the conversion to metric measures in some countries and its interpretations must have intimidated many a good cook.

Weights are given in the recipes only for ingredients such as meats, fish, poultry, and some vegetables. Though a few grams/ounces one way or another will not affect the success of your dish.

Though recipes have been tested using the Australian Standard 250mL cup, 20mL tablespoon, and 5mL teaspoon, they will work just as well with the US and Canadian 8 fl oz cup, or the UK 300mL cup. We have used graduated cup measures in preference to tablespoon measures so that proportions are always the same. Where tablespoon measures have been given, these are not crucial measures, so using the smaller tablespoon of the US or UK will not affect the recipe's success. At least we all agree on the teaspoon size.

For breads, cakes, and pastries, the only area which might cause concern is where eggs are used, as proportions will then vary. If working with a 250mL or 300mL cup, use large eggs (65g/2¼ oz), adding a little more liquid to the recipe for 300mL cup measures if it seems necessary. Use the medium-sized eggs (55g/2oz) with 8 fl oz cup measure. A graduated set of measuring cups and spoons is recommended, the cups in particular for measuring dry ingredients. Remember to level such ingredients to ensure their accuracy.

English measures

All measurements are similar to Australian with two exceptions: the English cup measures 300mL/10½ fl oz, whereas the Australian cup measure 250mL/8¾ fl oz. The English tablespoon (the Australian dessertspoon) measures 14.8mL/½ fl oz against the Australian tablespoon of 20mL/¾ fl oz.

American measures

The American reputed pint is 16 fl oz, a quart is equal to 32 fl oz and the American gallon, 128 fl oz. The Imperial measurement is 20 fl oz to the pint, 40 fl oz a quart and 160 fl oz one gallon. The American tablespoon is equal to 14.8 mL/½ fl oz, the teaspoon is 5 mL/⅙ fl oz. The cup measure is 250 mL/8¾ fl oz, the same as Australia.

Dry measures

All the measures are level, so when you have filled a cup or spoon, level it off with the edge of a knife. The scale below is the "cook's equivalent"; it is not an exact conversion of metric to imperial measurement. To calculate the exact metric equivalent yourself, multiply ounces by 28.349523 to obtain grams, or divide 28.349523 grams to obtain ounces.

Metric	Imperial
g = grams	oz = ounces
kg = kilograms	lb = pound
15g	½ oz
20g	⅔ oz
30g	1 oz
55g	2 oz
85g	3 oz
115g	4 oz/¼ lb
125g	4½ oz
140/145g	5 oz
170g	6 oz
200g	7 oz
225g	8 oz/½ lb
315g	11 oz
340g	12 oz/¾ lb
370g	13 oz
400g	14 oz
425g	15 oz
455g	16 oz/1 lb
1,000g/1kg	35.3 oz/2.2 lb
1.5kg	3.3 lb

Oven temperatures

The Celsius temperatures given here are not exact; they have been rounded off and are given as a guide only. Follow the manufacturer's temperature guide, relating it to oven description given in the recipe. Remember gas ovens are hottest at the top, electric ovens at the bottom, and convection-fan forced ovens are usually even throughout. We included Regulo numbers for gas cookers which may assist.
To convert °C to °F, multiply °C by 9, and divide by 5 then add 32.

Oven temperatures

	C°	F°	Gas regulo
Very slow	120	250	1
Slow	150	300	2
Moderately slow	160	325	3
Moderate	180	350	4
Moderately hot	190-200	370-400	5-6
Hot	210-220	410-440	6-7
Very hot	230	450	8
Super hot	250-290	475-500	9-10

Cake dish sizes

metric	imperial
15 cm	6 in
18 cm	7 in
20 cm	8 in
23 cm	9 in

Loaf dish sizes

metric	imperial
23x12 cm	9x5 in
25x8 cm	10x3 in
28x18 cm	11x7 in

Liquid measures

metric mL millilitres	imperial fl oz fluid ounce	cup and spoon
5mL	$\frac{1}{6}$ fl oz	1 teaspoon
20mL	$\frac{2}{3}$ fl oz	1 tablespoon
30mL	1 fl oz plus 2 teaspoons	1 tablespoon
55mL	2 fl oz	$\frac{1}{4}$ cup
85mL	3 fl oz	
115mL	4 fl oz	$\frac{1}{2}$ cup
125mL	$4\frac{1}{2}$ fl oz	
150mL	$5\frac{1}{4}$ fl oz	
170mL	6 fl oz	$\frac{3}{4}$ cup
225mL	8 fl oz	1 cup
300mL	$10\frac{1}{2}$ fl oz	
370mL	13 fl oz	
400mL	14 fl oz	$1\frac{3}{4}$ cups
455mL	16 fl oz	2 cups
570mL	20 fl oz	$2\frac{1}{2}$ cups
1 litre	35.3 fl oz	4 cups

Cup measurements

One cup is equal to the following weights.

	Metric	Imperial
Almonds, flaked	85g	3 oz
Almonds, slivered, ground	125g	$4\frac{1}{2}$ oz
Almonds, kernel	155g	$5\frac{1}{2}$ oz
Apples, dried, chopped	125g	$4\frac{1}{2}$ oz
Apricots, dried, chopped	190g	$6\frac{3}{4}$ oz
Breadcrumbs, packet	125g	$4\frac{1}{2}$ oz
Breadcrumbs, soft	55g	2 oz
Cheese, grated	115g	4 oz
Choc bits	$155\frac{1}{2}$g	5 oz
Coconut, desiccated	90g	3 oz
Cornflakes	30g	1 oz
Currants	$155\frac{1}{2}$g	5 oz
Flour	115g	4 oz
Fruit, dried (mixed, sultanas etc)	170g	6 oz
Ginger, crystallized, glace	250g	8 oz
Honey, treacle, golden syrup	315g	11 oz
Mixed peel	225g	8 oz
Nuts, chopped	115g	4 oz
Prunes, chopped	225g	8 oz
Rice, cooked	155g	$5\frac{1}{2}$ oz
Rice, uncooked	225g	8 oz
Rolled oats	90g	3 oz
Sesame seeds	115g	4 oz
Shortening (butter, margarine)	225g	8 oz
Sugar, brown	155g	$5\frac{1}{2}$ oz
Sugar, granulated or caster	225g	8 oz
Sugar, sifted icing	155g	$5\frac{1}{2}$ oz
Wheatgerm	60g	2 oz

Length

Some of us still have trouble converting imperial length to metric. In this scale, measures have been rounded off to the easiest-to-use and most acceptable figures. To obtain the exact metric equivalent in converting inches to centimeters, multiply inches by 2.54 whereby 1 inch equals 25.4 millimeters and 1 millimeter equals 0.03937 inches.

Metric mm=millimetres cm=centimetres	Imperial in = inches ft = feet
5 mm, 0.5 cm	$\frac{1}{4}$ in
10 mm, 1.0 cm	$\frac{1}{2}$ in
20 mm, 2.0 cm	$\frac{3}{4}$ in
2.5 cm	1 in
5 cm	2 in
$7\frac{1}{2}$ cm	3 in
10 cm	4 in
$12\frac{1}{2}$ cm	5 in
15 cm	6 in
18 cm	7 in
20 cm	8 in
23 cm	9 in
25 cm	10 in
28 cm	11 in
30 cm	12 in, 1ft

Index